*Ask and seek and your
heart will be big enough
to receive Him and keep
Him as your own.*

Mother Teresa

101 ways to talk to God

Sherry Morris

SPIRIT PRESS

101 Ways to Talk to God
ISBN: 1-40372-018-5

Published in 2006 by Spirit Press, an imprint of Dalmatian Press, LLC.
Copyright © 2006 Dalmatian Press, LLC. Franklin, Tennessee 37067.

Editor: Lila Empson
Cover and Text Design: Whisner Design Group

06 07 08 09 QSR 10 9 8 7 6 5 4 3 2 1

Printed in Canada

14936

*It is God to whom
and with whom we
travel, and while He
is the End of our
journey, He is also at
every stopping place.*

Elisabeth Elliot

Contents

Introduction

Become a Little Child .... #1

Shoot Straight to God's Heart .... #2

Open the Door for God .... #3

Encounter God Through Prayer .... #4

Be Yourself When You Pray .... #5

Try the Oldies but Goodies .... #6

Go on a Joyful Journey .... #7

Count Your Blessings .... #8

Make an Appointment with God .... #9

Make Holy Gestures .... #10

Know to Whom You Are Talking .... #11

Keep on the Sunny Side .... #12

Pray a Scripture .... #13

Make a Promise Book .... #14

Be Honest with God .... #15

Forgive Yourself .... #16

Make God Smile .... #17

Prioritize for Prayer .... #18

Find God in Unexpected Places .... #19

Look for Everyday Parables .... #20

Forgive and Be Free .... #21

Be God's Reflection .... #22

Be Thirsty for Water and Hungry for Fruit ...... #23

Consider the Possibilities .... #24

Embrace God's Love .... #25

Accept God's Gifts .... #26

Grab Hold Like a Child .... #27

Hold Up Your Candle .... #28

Be Creative in Prayer .... #29

Stop and Open Your Spiritual Eyes .... #30

Run the Race to Win .... #31

Imagine Big in Prayer .... #32

Make "God Bless You" a Prayer .... #33

People-Watch with a Purpose .... #34

Celebrate Your Supper .... #35

Begin Feeling Blessed .... #36

Ask If There Is More .... #37

Discover the Paradox of Praise .... #38

Go Online and Pray .... #39

Share the Joy .... #40

Pray Day by Day .... #41

Handle a Bad Day with Prayer .... #42

Welcome a Sleepless Night .... #43

Give a Precious Gift .... #44

Listen to the Crickets .... #45

Give Yourself a Spiritual Makeover .... #46

Engage Your Mind .... #47

Discover the Power of Words .... #48

Pray As If God Is Near .... #49

Contents continued...

Listen to a Child Pray . . . . #50
Catch a Glimpse of God . . . . #51
Pray a Psalm . . . . #52
Be Grateful for Grace . . . . #53
Reach Across Time . . . . #54
Get Your Exercise . . . . #55
Believe in a Coming Spring . . . . #56
Ask a Silly Question . . . . #57
Pray Anytime and Anywhere . . . . #58
Impact Others While You Are Here . . . . #59
Make a Difference Today . . . . #60
Ask for a Greater Measure . . . . #61
Carry Someone's Burden . . . . #62
Be Short and Sweet . . . . #63
Develop a Heart Habit . . . . #64
Make Delightful Lists . . . . #65
Have a Split Conversation . . . . #66
Give God Your Life Goals . . . . #67
Take a Cleansing Bath . . . . #68
Release Your Worries . . . . #69
Find a New Way . . . . #70
Share a Gift of Grace . . . . #71
Learn from Your Experience . . . . #72
Imagine Heaven . . . . #73
Pray Like Hannah . . . . #74
Get a Whiff and Pray . . . . #75

Stand Together .... #76

Do Your Work for God .... #77

Get in Rhythm .... #78

Inspire an Everyday Hero .... #79

Stand Up for Justice .... #80

Give Legs to God's Love .... #81

Listen for the Right Time .... #82

Be Willing to Give .... #83

Fill Someone's Shoes .... #84

Host a "Care Aware" Party .... #85

Try a Sticky-Note Method .... #86

Be Inspired by Faith Heroes .... #87

Take a Prayer Walk .... #88

Hold Someone's Hand .... #89

Take on a Tough Issue .... #90

Pray as You Pay .... #91

Ask for a Life Verse .... #92

Pray Your ABC's .... #93

Ask for a Miracle .... #94

Pray Without Pretense .... #95

Count the Ways .... #96

Applaud God .... #97

Ask If Now Is the Time .... #98

Be Enriched Through Fasting .... #99

State Your Family's Purpose .... #100

Look to the Morning Star .... #101

Introduction

Prayer is talking with God. It is an expression of a love relationship between God and people of faith. Elizabeth Barrett Browning said in her famous sonnet, "How do I love thee? Let me count the ways." In a relationship, ways of expressing love are as many and varied as the kindred spirits involved. Count the meditations that follow as 101 ways to approach loving conversations with God. Enjoy each one as an idea to help you begin or deepen a loving relationship with him.

Prayer is not only talking to God. It is listening to him speak. How does he love you? His ways also are too numerous to count. God's creativity goes beyond anything you can ask or imagine. To hear God speak, you have to be willing to listen and to be open to all the possibilities of God. Begin today to count the ways you can express your love for God. Delight in the countless ways he shows his love for you.

You pay God a compliment by asking great things of him.

Saint Theresa of Avila

Call to Me, and I will answer you, and show you great and mighty things, which you do not know.

Jeremiah 33:3 NKJV

#1

Become a Little Child

Jesus taught his followers about the kingdom of heaven. He explained that they needed childlike faith to experience the kingdom of heaven on earth. Feel the difference that becoming like a little child makes in prayer. Talk to him with childlike confidence and expect him to bless you.

Jesus offered a lesson to back up his words. His followers didn't think they should allow children to bother him, and they tried to send them away. Jesus said he wanted the children to come to him, and he blessed them. Run to him with the confidence of a child and ask for a blessing. Be assured that he will bless you.

child

> *[Jesus] said, "I'm telling you, once and for all, that unless you return to square one and start over like children, you're not even going to get a look at the kingdom, let alone get in."*
>
> Matthew 18:3 MSG

≫ Picture yourself as a small child climbing up on Jesus' lap. Touch his face. Feel his arms around you. Know he wants to bless you.

#2

Shoot Straight to God's Heart

The biggest problem in prayer is how to let go and let God.

Glenn Clark

heart

In an unskilled archer's hands, an arrow often doesn't get close to hitting the mark. The first step in learning to shoot is simply to pull back the bowstring and let the arrow go. Discover today that shooting straight to God's heart requires no skill and no practice.

Prayer is an arrow that never misses its mark. No matter how short, how long, how well phrased, or how you may speak them on the fly, words of prayer always reach the heart of God. Be confident in how you pray. Let the prayers go from your heart straight to God. God will take over from there.

>> Whatever is on your heart today, talk to God about it. Know that your words hit their mark and that God feels what's on your heart.

#3

Open the Door for God

Are you confident you know what's best for the people in your life? God knows. Ask him what is best. Seek what God wants to do in someone you love, no matter what the challenge or circumstance. Knock on heaven's door and pray for God's best for those you love.

Prayer opens the door for God to work in people's lives. The best you can do for anyone is to invite God to make his unmistakable presence known. Believe that experiencing God is more than you can ask or imagine for anyone. Ask, seek, and knock through prayer on behalf of the people you love.

open

> *Ask, and you will receive; seek, and you will find; knock, and the door will be opened to you.*
>
> Matthew 7:7 GNT

>> Think of a loved one. Spend time in prayer for the one who is on your mind. Be confident that your prayers make a difference.

#4

Encounter God Through Prayer

> *We know him through the sixth sense that God has given every person — that ability to believe.*
>
> Billy Graham

prayer

Even if you have never before experienced God, you can encounter him today. How do you have an encounter with God? Pray. Encountering God is as straightforward as saying a prayer. The act of prayer itself is an acknowledgment that you understand you are not alone in the universe. This understanding is no mere coincidence or psychological phenomenon. God created and designed you so that you could discover him.

God is there to hear the words spoken from your heart. Just talk to him. Ask him to help you discover the ability to believe. Have an encounter with God.

>> If you are in the car, turn off the radio and pray. If you are at home or at work, find a quiet moment to speak to the One who created you.

#5

Be Yourself When You Pray

Everyone has a different learning style. Some people learn best through talking and writing. Others learn best through listening or doing. Because God made people to learn in different ways, it makes sense that he would allow each one to converse with him in ways that are unique to each person. Be yourself when you pray.

yourself

If you learn through written words, try journaling your prayers. If you learn by listening, try praying out loud or singing your prayers. If you learn by doing, try making your actions a prayer to please God. He designed you to pray best in a style that's uniquely you.

> *You, LORD, are our Father. We are nothing but clay, but you are the potter who molded us.*
>
> Isaiah 64:8 CEV

>> Look at yourself in a mirror and smile. Pray the way God made you. Be open to expressing your heart to God in new ways.

#6

Try the Oldies but Goodies

A good prayer,
though often used, is
still fresh and fair in
the eyes of heaven.

Thomas Fuller

oldies

You may sometimes feel the need for divine inspiration just to talk with God, or you may feel at a loss for words in knowing what to say. Try praying from a prayer book. Prayer books contain conversations with God that transcend the range of human thought and emotion. The words may speak the thoughts you would have if you could just put your thoughts into words. Pray these oldies but goodies.

The difference between talking to God and saying a prayer is the faith of the heart that speaks it. Even if you borrow some words from someone else, know that God listens to your faith.

≫ Invest in *The Book of Common Prayer*. When you can't think of what to say to God, let the prayers from ages past speak for you.

#7

Go on a Joyful Journey

Get set for a journey. Step into prayer with all the expectation of beginning a trip to a new destination. Prayer is the vehicle that carries you about your business here on earth. Prayer carries you from situation to situation and around the curves. Prayer carries you through the traffic jams and onto the open highway.

A hope-filled journey with God begins when you become aware that he *is* and desire to be closer to him. The journey begins when you tell him with a prayer that you want to travel through this life with him. Go on the joyful journey.

joy

> *Be joyful always, pray at all times, be thankful in all circumstances. This is what God wants from you in your life in union with Christ Jesus.*
>
> 1 Thessalonians 5:16–18 GNT

>> Thank God for the traveling privilege of prayer. Delight in knowing that he is with you all the way.

#8

Count Your Blessings

> *If we let him, an exuberant freedom to bless others will flourish.*
>
> Bruce Wilkinson

count

A hymn written in the mid-nineteenth century, "Count Your Blessings," still graces the pages of many hymnals today. "Count your blessings, name them one by one," instructs the lyrics. The hymn's message is timeless: even if you're discouraged and you think all is lost, just think about the good things in life and see what God has done.

Have you counted your blessings today? Try naming them one by one. Thank God for the many gifts he's given you. Share with others the joy having a blessed life gives you. Pray for your life to become a song of blessing to everyone you meet.

≫ Make a list of your blessings. On a day when things are not going well for you, look at your list and be reminded of all the blessings you enjoy.

#9

Make an Appointment with God

Do you have important clients that you always make time for? Are these clients the ones who can benefit you most financially or who can help you reach your professional goals? God is your best resource in all endeavors, including business and your daily affairs. Make time for that most important appointment with God today. It will make a difference in everything you do.

An appointment with God is time well spent. God will give you insight and inspiration; he will give you a fresh look at your problems and challenges. Meet with him for provision and guidance in all things.

time

> *You will keep on guiding me with your counsel, leading me to a glorious destiny.*
>
> Psalm 73:24 NLT

>> Assign time on your appointment calendar for you to spend with God. Bring the challenges you face to him, and listen for his counsel throughout your day.

#10

Make Holy Gestures

> *A little thing is a little thing, but faithfulness in a little thing is a great thing.*
>
> J. Hudson Taylor

gesture

Some people bow their heads when they pray. Others shut their eyes. In a church setting, people may kneel. Each of these gestures creates a posture for prayer. None of them are necessary to talk to God. Just a thought or a deed turned heavenward can be a holy gesture. Make many holy gestures as you go through your day.

Smile at someone you don't know. Pick up some trash along a roadside. Speak a word of encouragement to a coworker. Do things with a heart to please God, and your words and actions will become holy gestures of your faith in him.

>> Think of an ordinary task. Reflect on the Scripture "Whatever you do, work at it with all your heart, as though you were working for the Lord and not for people" (Colossians 3:23 GNT).

#11

Know to Whom You Are Talking

Some people think prayer is only an inner, self-comforting dialogue. Talking to yourself may clarify how you feel about a circumstance or issue, but talking to God is more. Prayer is a way to speak to the Source of wisdom. Have a prayer dialogue with the One who can make a difference. Know to whom you are talking.

If you are talking to the God of all wisdom, there is nothing you can't ask. He doesn't just have the answers; he *is* the answer. When you begin to understand this, you begin to understand God. He wants to talk to you. Talk to him. He's listening.

know

> *If any of you needs wisdom, you should ask God for it. He is generous and enjoys giving to all people, so he will give you wisdom.*
>
> James 1:5 NCV

≫ Approach God with a sense of awe and wonder. Know that you have the ear of the Wisdom of the universe.

#12

Keep on the Sunny Side

> *To love and be loved is to feel the sunshine from both sides.*
>
> David Viscott

sunny

Song lyrics brightened the spirits of those who faced life's difficulties during the Great Depression. "Keep on the Sunny Side of Life" encouraged people to rise above the troubled times. The words suggested looking for the small joys to be found in each day. This is great advice for living. Look for the sunny side of life.

If you need help finding the joyful, happy side of life, ask God to reveal to you the joy that comes from lifting the hearts of those around you. Nothing brings sunshine to life like the joy that comes from bringing joy to others. Bask in the sunny side of life.

≫ Look for someone who needs a lift today, and find a small kindness you can do. Discover the joy that comes from lifting the hearts of others.

#13

Pray a Scripture

Saint Benedict, the founder and namesake of the Benedictine monastic order, taught the practice of prayer by meditation. He spoke Scripture aloud and placed emphasis on different phrases and words within the verse. He encouraged his followers to meditate on Scripture and allow the words of Scripture to reveal something God wanted them to know.

Praying a Scripture is a good way to talk to God. Choose a Scripture. Where it is appropriate, personalize it with your name. As you repeat it, emphasize different words within the verse. Think about it throughout the day. Talk to God about the words, and wait for understanding.

scripture

> *Your word is a lamp to my feet and a light for my path.*
>
> Psalm 119:105 NIV

>> Choose a verse that you want to understand better. Pray this Scripture often throughout your day. Let God speak to you.

#14

Make a Promise Book

> *The future is as bright as the promises of God.*
>
> Adoniram Judson

promise

Scrapbooks contain photos that often become chronicles of a family's history. Tuck more than just photographs into the pages of birthday parties, sporting triumphs, and fun days together. Add God's promises from Scripture. Tell God you desire his blessings on your family's future.

On a baby's page, write a blessing such as "The LORD bless you and keep you" (Numbers 6:24 NKJV). On a graduate's page, include a promise such as "Delight yourself also in the LORD, and He shall give you the desires of your heart" (Psalm 37:4 NKJV). Add God's promises to your pages of family history. Ask God to bless your future together.

≫ Start a scrapbook of blessings today. Include your personal prayers for your family. Brighten your scrapbook with promises you have prayed for the future.

#15

Be Honest with God

Are you angry? Do you suffer with past hurts? Say so. You can't tell God anything he doesn't already know. Be honest with him. Just as you would tell a friend about your feelings, feel free to tell God. God appreciates your openness. Approach him honestly.

Even Jesus expressed doubt in the garden where he prayed. Jesus was honest about his feelings. And when he voiced a desire to let the cup pass, he was given strength to complete his mission. So go ahead and cry out against the injustices, hurts, and disappointments in your life. You cannot offend God with honesty.

honest

> *O my people, trust in him at all times. Pour out your heart to him.*
>
> Psalm 62:8 NLT

≫ Write God an honest letter. Tell him what you think and feel. Expect honest answers from him. He sees the big picture in your purpose for being.

feel

101 ways to

expect

discover

seek

knock

talk to God

think

believe

encounter

#16

Forgive Yourself

> *God paints in many colors, but he never paints so gorgeously as when he paints in white.*
>
> G. K. Chesterton

forgive

The color white represents purity and cleanliness. Consider whether you would choose white to describe how you feel about yourself. Or whether you would choose some other color because you feel past events have left your life stained. God is more than willing to forgive you of your past. His will is to forgive you. His forgiveness will clothe you in white again.

Sometimes the hardest part of receiving God's forgiveness is being able to forgive yourself. Accept God's forgiveness today for past mistakes and failures. His love will dissolve any stain you make on your life. Forgive yourself. Ask him to dress you in white again.

≫ Cut a square of white cloth and stretch it in a photograph frame. Place it where you can see it. Let it remind you that you are forgiven.

#17

Make God Smile

Vocal and instrumental songs of worship and praise are beautiful and traditional ways to please God. Music is one way to worship. So also is prayer. God finds the prayerful music of your heart delightful. Give yourself fully in worship. Pray from the heart. Make God smile through your joyful expressions of prayer and praise.

Envision God's response when your thoughts turn toward him. Express how you feel about the wonder and awe of his love. Involve all of who you are in your prayer and praise. Is there anything more important to do today than to make God smile?

smile

> *Love the Lord your God with all your heart and with all your soul and with all your mind and with all your strength.*
>
> Mark 12:30 NIV

>> Put in a worship tape or CD while in the car and sing at the top of your lungs.

#18

Prioritize for Prayer

> *Don't just pray when you feel like it. Have an appointment with the King and keep it.*
>
> Corrie ten Boom

prioritize

Do you have an organizer or a PDA? Do you fill it with appointments, events, and day-to-day reminders of things to do? If you are like most people, your life's work keeps you busy. The need for some organization is pressing.

Scrutinize your daily calendar. Do you find you are just too busy to pray? If so, then you are just too busy. Think about how you might better spend your time so you have some quiet moments for prayer. Are there some unnecessary activities that keep you from quality time with God? Drop the unnecessary for the important. Prioritize the activities of your life for prayer.

≫ Buy a devotional guide at a bookstore. Use it. At the end of your week, see how spending time with God makes a difference in you.

#19

Find God in Unexpected Places

A cathedral becomes a place to experience God's presence only when people enter it and expect to find him. For the psalmist David, a pond in a pasture became a cathedral. Next to still waters, David found the One who restored his soul. A cathedral can be any time or any place that allows you to be still and know God.

Look for God today. Sitting in a porch swing looking at a sunset or enjoying some solitude in a bubble bath can be an unexpected opportunity to be still and seek the presence of God. If you are expecting to find him, a cathedral is just a prayer away.

find

> *I will personally go with you, Moses. I will give you rest— everything will be fine for you.*
>
> Exodus 33:14 NLT

≫ Do something different today. Keep your eyes and heart open for a new place that inspires you to meet God.

#20

Look for Everyday Parables

Everything happening, great and small, is a parable whereby God speaks to us, and the art of life is to get the message.

Malcolm Muggeridge

look

A parable is a story that conveys a truth. Jesus used parables to help his followers understand his teachings. By calling attention to simple moments and circumstances, he spoke to the heart of earthly concerns and placed them in a much broader perspective—a heavenly one. Look for everyday parables to see how God might be speaking to you.

Is there a story being told through events in your life? Ask God to help you have eyes to see and ears to hear his message for you. Be open to seeing direction for your life in the smallest of happenings. Look for the everyday parable.

≫ Summarize a story from your life. Think of the central truth your story conveys. Ask God if this parable is meant to teach you.

#21

Forgive and Be Free

To speak intimately with God requires that you forgive others just as he forgives you. In only one place does the Bible record that Jesus ever wrote anything. As he wrote, he offered a life lesson that promised spiritual freedom for all involved. Forgive and be free.

Jesus said as he wrote on the ground that if anyone was without sin, then that person should throw the first stone. Since no one is without sin, no one threw a stone. If someone has hurt you, ask God to help you forgive that person today. Thank God that he also forgives you.

freedom

> *Forgive us our sins, for we also forgive everyone who sins against us. And lead us not into temptation.*
>
> Luke 11:4 NIV

≫ Read John 8:3–11. Write a note of forgiveness to someone today. Release a past hurt. Walk away free.

#22

Be God's Reflection

> *What we love we will grow to resemble.*
>
> Saint Bernard of Clairvaux

reflect

God is love. God is peace. God is joy. He designed you to be a mirror of his holy nature. To be a reflection of God, you must first love him. Then discover how he created you to illuminate his love, peace, and joy. Ask God to help you live to be his reflection.

When the world seems like a scary place, when problems seem too big to overcome, when there is more wrong than right in your universe, God's love within you can reflect his joy and peace no matter what the circumstances. Love God, and you'll begin to resemble who he is.

>> Tell God you love him. Be specific about why. Ask to be his holy reflection in something that happens today.

#23

Be Thirsty for Water and Hungry for Fruit

A spiritual harvest comes from planting seeds that bear spiritual fruit. From good seeds come good fruit. Purposefully plant good works and sow good seeds in your life. Spread love, joy, peace, patience, kindness, goodness, faithfulness, gentleness, and self-control to others. Discover how prayer is living water that gives life to a spiritual harvest.

Ask God to help you plant spiritual seeds today. Plant a seed of kindness. Sow a fruit of the spirit. Water the fruit of your life through prayer. Harvest the fruit of God's love in you. Reap the joy of God. Be thirsty for prayer and hungry for its fruit.

thirst

He satisfies those who are thirsty and fills the hungry with good things.

Psalm 107:9 GNT

≫ Give a friend a book you've enjoyed on prayer. Ask later if he or she enjoyed it. Plant a seed to grow in someone you know.

#24

Consider the Possibilities

> *Ask and seek and your heart will be big enough to receive Him and keep Him as your own.*
>
> Mother Teresa

consider

Prayer is much more than a wonderful, mysterious thing. Sometimes it evokes an image. Sometimes it becomes a state of being. Descriptions of prayer help you understand the wonderful intimacy you can have with God. Think about what prayer is.

Sometimes it may seem hard to find the right words to explain prayer. Think about how you can describe it. Here are some examples: Prayer is a snug bed on a stormy night. Prayer is a compass to chart a course. Prayer is a walk under the stars with a friend. Ask God to help you describe what prayer is. Open your heart to the possibilities of God.

≫ Make a list of descriptions that are particularly relevant for your life. Draw them from your routine experiences. Share your prayer descriptions with a friend.

#25

Embrace God's Love

Someone once asked a great theologian how he would summarize Scripture. Expecting a long answer about the Book that has had an unparalleled impact on the world, the audience was surprised by the theologian's reply. He answered with the words of a child's song, "Jesus loves me! this I know." How exciting to embrace the love that changed the world.

Be assured that God gave his message in Scripture for you. Pray a prayer of praise for a love that is large enough to reach around the earth and yet still includes you. And as surprising as this truth is, all anyone has to do to receive God's love is to return his embrace.

embrace

> *Come near to God,*
> *and God will come*
> *near to you.*
>
> James 4:8 NCV

≫ If you never learned it or can't remember it, find the song "Jesus Loves Me" in a hymnal. Sing it with a heart that accepts the simple truth of God's love.

#26

Accept God's Gifts

Scripture is God's gift to us to show us how to get the most happiness out of life.

Saint Augustine

gifts

God's promises bring happiness and good to those who believe. From Genesis to Revelation, the promises of God are strewn throughout all the books of the Bible. To find out what he has promised, read Scripture; and to claim his promises, pray. Believe the promises are yours and make them your own.

Even if you pray a promise every day this year, you can't pray all the promises of God. Many Bible editions list God's promises to make them easy to find. Look for promises that speak to your heart. Pray the promises for you. Accept the gift of God's promises.

≫ Put your own name in a promise you pray. Know that the promise is yours.

#27

Grab Hold Like a Child

Think about a child riding Daddy's foot. Transported with joy, children hold on tight and laugh. They know they're safe and that nothing will happen to them. If frightened, children know instinctively to grab Daddy and hang on. Prayer is a gift from God, your heavenly Father, and you can hang on to him through prayer.

It's a joy to ride through life with someone who loves you and wants to walk with you. When things get tough, know you have a place to go for comfort and assurance. Envision yourself as his child. See God. Grab hold and hang on.

grab

> *GOD is our refuge and strength, always ready to help in times of trouble.*
>
> Psalm 46:1 NLT

≫ Check a concordance or an online Bible search, such as biblegateway.com or crosswalk.com, for verses about God's comfort.

#28

Hold Up Your Candle

> *Give light, and the darkness will disappear of itself.*
>
> Desiderius Erasmus

hold

A popular song on the contemporary Christian music charts a few years ago became known as "The Candle Song." The lyrics, which told listeners to take their candles and go light their world, challenged listeners to be a light for God in the world. Prayer is the spark that lights your candle for God.

In a dark room, a candle's light makes all the difference. The tiny flicker of prayer lights up the dark places of life. Whatever you face today, you can have the light of prayer and shine it for all to see. Hold up your candle. Ask God to light the flame.

≫ Sit in a quiet, dark room. Light a scented candle. Put on some calming music. Enjoy special time to be alone with God.

#29

Be Creative in Prayer

Since ancient times, people have used the fragrance of incense to call others to devotional activities. The fragrances mentioned in the Bible include cinnamon, dill, mint, cumin, and parsley. Share these fragrant garden gifts as a creative way to invite others to think about God.

Do you want to offer inspirational thoughts to friends? Bundle and tie some fresh herbs with ribbon. Attach the herbs to decorative cards printed with a favorite Scripture and the verse: "Taste and see that the LORD is good" (Psalm 34:8 NLT). Pray your gifts will help friends see God's word as fresh inspiration for their lives.

create

> *Live a life of love, just as Christ loved us and gave himself up for us as a fragrant offering and sacrifice to God.*
>
> Ephesians 5:2 NIV

≫ Ask God to help you see creativity as a gift you can use in many ways to serve him.

#30

Stop and Open Your Spiritual Eyes

> *It is God to whom and with whom we travel, and while He is the End of our journey, He is also at every stopping place.*
>
> Elisabeth Elliot

open

Prayer is part of your spiritual journey. Every parent who has traveled with children knows the incessant question, "Are we there yet?" Part of the challenge of being a parent is to help children learn to spend the time enjoying the sights along the way. Ask yourself if you are in a hurry as you travel through your busy days. If so, slow down and look around you with renewed vision to take in all there is to see.

Ask God today for new spiritual insight. Learn to appreciate what appears on the horizon. Don't just pass the time you have on life's journey. Sit down and reflect. Open your spiritual eyes.

≫ Relax in a hammock. Listen to the birds. Enjoy a sunset. Drink a second cup of coffee. Slow down long enough to see what God has to say to you.

#31

Run the Race to Win

The mother of world-renowned painter Picasso once told him, "If you become a soldier, you'll be a general. If you become a monk, you'll be pope." Picasso told this tongue in cheek as he told his listeners, "I became a painter and wound up as 'Picasso.'"

Be certain and be convinced in your heart that you are uniquely gifted and created for something special. Are you using your God-given gifts to the fullest? Ask God if you are running to win the race he wants you to run. Seek to discover all your gifts, and desire to do your best. Get in the race to win.

run

> *Remember that in a race everyone runs, but only one person gets the prize.*
>
> 1 Corinthians 9:24
> NLT

≫ Make it a goal to try a new skill or hobby. Tell God you want a passion to run and to win every race he has planned for you.

consider

101 ways to

choose

forgive

give

envision

talk to God

sing

express

scrutinize

#32

Imagine Big in Prayer

> *You pay God a compliment by asking great things of him.*
>
> Saint Theresa of Avila

imagine

God can do great things. From the largest to the smallest detail of your life, God is over all. Though he's concerned with the simple day-to-day things, he invites you to believe he can do big things in your life as well. You can ask great things of God. He is up to the challenge.

What are you concerned about today? Are you starting something new? Or did you simply lose your keys? Either situation is cause to pray. Give him all, great or small. Know that you can ask him for more than you can imagine. Be free to imagine big.

≫ Imagine some great what-ifs. Ask God if these are possibilities he has for you. Choose one to pray about today.

#33

Make "God Bless You" a Prayer

make

The practice of saying "God bless you" began as more than just politeness. During the time of the Great Plague in seventeenth-century London, the expression was said as a prayer to stay well. Make your "God bless you" more than just something you say. Make it both a prayer and something you do.

Next time you hear a sneeze, say "May God bless you." Make your smile be a blessing for the person. Speak an extra word of kindness. Be more than just polite in responding to a sneeze. Speak your blessing to be a blessing. Ask God to use your words to help others feel blessed.

> *I pray that you may enjoy good health and that all may go well with you, even as your soul is getting along well.*
>
> 3 John 2 NIV

≫ Keep a "blessing" candy jar. Attach to the wrapped candy written blessings, like "May God grant you health today." Offer your treats when someone sneezes.

#34

People-Watch with a Purpose

> *To love anyone is nothing else than to wish that person good.*
>
> Saint Thomas Aquinas

watch

The next time you are at a shopping mall or another place where many people walk by, stop and people-watch with a purpose. As you watch, pick out a person in the crowd who looks as if he or she needs a prayer. Share God's love today through prayer. Pray good things for the person you notice.

Believe you can make a difference for the person you see. Pray for no reason other than the desire to bring good to someone else. If you see an opportunity for kindness, be kind. Do more than just watch people pass by. Pick a person to pray for.

≫ If the person you've prayed for comes back your way, pray for him or her a second time.

#35

Celebrate Your Supper

In the comic strip "Peanuts," Snoopy does a happy dance when supper is served. Charles Schulz did a number of cartoons about what made Snoopy happy. For the famous beagle, supper was just another reason to dance. Have an attitude of gratitude for good things in life. Celebrate your supper.

Thank God for the provision he's given. Are you eating a fresh ear of corn or a homegrown tomato? Bite the corn with relish and delight in its sweetness. Savor a tomato's juiciness. Be happy that you have plenty of good, nourishing food. Thank God for all the good things you enjoy.

celebrate

How blessed the people who have all this! How blessed the people who have GOD for God!

Psalm 144:15 MSG

≫ Try a new recipe. Set the table festively. Gather your family for a thankful prayer, and enjoy your supper as a celebration of life.

#36

Begin Feeling Blessed

> *Grace is always given to those who are ready to give thanks for it.*
>
> Thomas à Kempis

begin

A great start gives your day momentum. Setting the tone can be as easy as choosing what you think about in the first few minutes. What better way to begin the day than with a prayer of praise? Begin with a good attitude and positive thoughts about the life God has given you.

Try an experiment. Wake up every day this week and give yourself twenty positive minutes. Pray with a heart of thanksgiving for all the good things in life. Refuse to think of anything negative. See if starting your day this way doesn't make the whole day go better. Begin blessed; end best.

≫ Make a top-ten list of positives in your life. Celebrate one or more of these from your list each day this week.

#37

Ask If There Is More

Let your birthday be an opportunity to offer God thanks for your life. Invite your family and friends to a different kind of celebration this year. Ask them to reflect with you on who you've been, what you are, and what they see you becoming in the future. Share your own dreams and aspirations. Make your birthday a celebration of you—past, present, and future.

You've been uniquely created and have a purpose for being here. Ask God if you are fulfilling his purposes for you. Make this birthday a time to celebrate all you are. Then ask God if there's more he wants you to be.

ask

> *Finish what you started in me, GOD. Your love is eternal—don't quit on me now.*
>
> Psalm 138:8 MSG

>> Mark the day of your birth on a calendar each month from January to December. Make that day a day to pray about God's purpose for your life.

#38

Discover the Paradox of Praise

> *A child of God should be a visible beatitude for joy and a living doxology for gratitude.*
>
> C. H. Spurgeon

p r a i s e

The doxology song invites people to "praise God from whom all blessings flow." Discover God's wonderful paradox of praise: When you praise God, you feel blessed. When you feel blessed, you praise God. Pray that your life will be a living doxology. Ask God to help you experience his wonderful paradox of praise.

Let today be a day to praise God and to feel the joy of his great love for you. Because today you feel his love and blessings, celebrate the joy of having a great God. Thank God that you experience praise and blessings. Live to help others discover his wonderful paradox of praise.

>> Make today a day to think of ten reasons you praise God. Praise God for all ten reasons.

#39

Go Online and Pray

Connecting with the Internet-jargon generation, a church sign read GOD ANSWERS KNEE-MAIL—a wordplay with a practical application. The Internet is a tool for many things. Why not make it a tool for prayer? With the click of a mouse, connect with others through the Internet and pray with and for them. By knee-mail or e-mail, God answers prayer.

E-mail your prayer to friends with a need to let them know you prayed for them. Find prayer sites to learn how to pray for causes you believe in. Visit a prayer chat room. Go online. Discover a new way to voice a prayer.

online

Call to Me, and I will answer you, and show you great and mighty things, which you do not know.

Jeremiah 33:3 NKJV

>> Visit a site like familylife.com to experience the dynamics of corporate prayer. Consider becoming a prayer partner.

#40

Share the Joy

> *Thanksgiving is good, but thanks-living is better.*
>
> Matthew Henry

share

A young man from an arid area of California visited Oklahoma. Standing on a porch, he was so awed by the sounds and sights of what the locals called a gullywasher that he woke his wife. Together they watched the storm. When the danger of lightning passed, they danced in the rain. Dripping and laughing, the young man said, "All this and you, too."

Like this young man, live a moment someone else might let pass by unnoticed. Do something special and unexpected with someone you love. Be creative. Thank God for the simple joy of life and having someone—friend, spouse, neighbor, coworker—with whom to share it.

≫ Pack a picnic for two. Plan a surprise trip. Find a moment of unbridled joy and say a heartfelt prayer of thanks for "all this and you, too."

#41

Pray Day by Day

Thomas Welch originally pasteurized grape juice to be used for Communion at his church. The year was 1869. A desire to create a drink suitable for a Communion table became a thriving business, and the name Welch's became known in most households. Because of the process Welch developed, many churches still serve grape juice at the Communion table.

Thank God for a different kind of process he created to make communion with him possible. Take the communion cup of prayer. Let God's name become part of your household. Thank him that he created prayer to give you the experience of day-by-day communion with him.

thank

> *Prayer keeps us in constant communion with God, which is the goal of our entire believing lives.*
>
> Beth Moore

≫ Go to a church communion service. Listen to the minister as he prepares to give communion. Prepare your own heart for communion with God.

#42

Handle a Bad Day with Prayer

Every tomorrow has two handles. We can take hold of the handle of anxiety or the handle of faith.

Henry Ward Beecher

handle

A bad day is a storm determined to beat you. A rumble of thunderous trouble may be followed by a torrent of dismal happenings and end with a splintering crack in a dream or goal. Ask God to help you get through your bad day. Let a bad day be what it is— an opportunity to grow.

Picture yourself as a broken tree after a storm. Know that God is faithful. Pray about unfortunate circumstances. Believe that tomorrow's promises grow from buds of a stronger and more resilient you. Thank God the sun never shines brighter than right after a storm. Handle a bad day with prayer.

>> Ask God to prune away any hurt, anger, or disappointment you feel. Ask if he is pruning you for changes he has in mind.

#43

Welcome a Sleepless Night

Ever had a night when you just couldn't sleep? Do something constructive with your time—talk to God. Bring him whatever is on your mind. Think about how he can use something as irritating as a sleepless night to bring something good to your life. Welcome sleeplessness as quality time with God.

Are you restless because of a problem? Give it to God. Are you sleepless because of some unfinished business? Let God help you work a plan to get through it. Troubled about a relationship? Pray about it. Let the peace of God pass over you. Even if you can't sleep, relax and rest in God's company.

welcome

> *When I remember You on my bed, I meditate on You in the night watches.*
> Psalm 63:6 NKJV

>> Journal your late-night reflections. Read your journal in the daytime and note how God uses your nighttime sleeplessness to give you daytime wisdom.

#44

Give a Precious Gift

> *The heart of the giver makes the gift precious.*
>
> Martin Luther

gift

A young child creates gifts for parents with care. Parents receive gifts with secret smiles and hearts full of love for the effort made, even though crooked cuts cross the paper and crayon marks stray over lines. Be childlike in prayer today. Think about God's secret smiles as you pray to live the best you know how. Know that his love for you goes beyond all your efforts.

Approach God with an open and loving heart. Offer him your best. Believe he is smiling at you. Know you are precious to him. Thank him for his loving patience with you.

>> Draw a picture for God. Color something from your life that you know would please him. Put your picture on your refrigerator as a reminder that you are growing in your relationship with God through prayer.

#45

Listen to the Crickets

Go outside on a warm summer night and just listen. The crickets, cicadas, or locusts (whatever is indigenous to your area) perform a constant chorus. Using the parts of their bodies designed for sound, they bless the world with their unmistakable night song. Learn a lesson from a cricket.

God also designed you to bless the world through the way he made you. Think about your unique God-given gifts and talents. Unlike the cricket, you have a choice whether or not to use them. Since you are made to bless others, ask God to show you how best to do this.

listen

> As each one has received a special gift, employ it in serving one another as good stewards of the manifold grace of God.
>
> 1 Peter 4:10 NASB

>> Are you patient, confident, creative, or persistent? Jot down ways you can use your special abilities or attributes for God.

#46

Give Yourself a Spiritual Makeover

> *Fix your attention on God. You'll be changed from the inside out.*
>
> Romans 12:2 MSG

give

Unlike a thirty-minute reality show, a spiritual makeover takes time. Just as a physical makeover changes the outer being to make an inner difference, different approaches to spiritual things can create a new, reenergized inner being. Plan your own spiritual makeover.

Begin with how you focus on God now. If you always pray by yourself, start praying with others. If you don't have a special place for prayer, create one. If you spend more time in service with people, spend more time in solitude, and vice versa. Ask God to help you make some changes in your habits to spiritually renew and energize you.

≫ Contemplate giving yourself a spiritual makeover. List your weak points that need to be strengthened. Then list your strong points that need to be enhanced.

#47

Engage Your Mind

Being a thinker in prayer means engaging your mind to analyze, reason, and discern God's truth about people or circumstances. If you let him, he can work in you to bring about needed changes in both you and the situation you face. Pray with your mind engaged. Ask God to reveal his heart for your situation.

Think about what might be causing ripples in relationships, and consider what could be causing wrinkles in circumstances. Ask God for solutions that leave everyone's self-esteem intact. Trust the insight he gives you. Engage your mind through prayer, and be open to the heart of God.

mind

Let the Spirit of God lead us into the intent of God's heart.

Watchman Nee

>> Think about circumstances you can pray for. Ask for the intent of God's heart to be at work. Be open to the changes God can make in and through you.

imagine

101 ways to

bless

share

pray

dance

talk to God

experiment

celebrate

praise

#48

Discover the Power of Words

Understanding your word brings light to the minds of ordinary people.

Psalm 119:130 CEV

words

Words have power to encourage and inspire. Is there a space in your home or office that you could fill with encouraging words? Create a word wall. Paint it. Cover it with corkboard. Or hang a magnet board with magnetic words or letters. Make some space for family, friends, or coworkers to find a source of encouragement and inspiration.

Write prayers of blessings for people you know who will look at your wall. Include Bible verses about prayer. Pray that your written words will make a mark on the life of someone you know. Ask God to use your wall to encourage others to think about him.

>> Read an inspirational book of quotes and Bible verses. Think about the way the words influence you.

#49

Pray As If God Is Near

A little boy left church one day knowing that his family was going on vacation the next Sunday. As his family pulled out of the parking lot, the little boy said, "Good-bye, church. Good-bye, Bible books. Good-bye, people. Good-bye, God." He paused and then said in a tone that revealed his awe at a new idea, "No, wait. God is going with us."

God is going with you on your life's journey. Be amazed and reassured by the knowledge that he is with you wherever you go. Think of his presence near you through the day. Pray as if he's in the room.

near

You need not cry very loudly; he is nearer to us than we think.

Brother Lawrence

≫ Sit in a chair and think about everything you are aware of around you. Feel God's presence. Thank him for being with you wherever you go.

#50

Listen to a Child Pray

> *From the mouth of infants and nursing babes You have established strength.*
>
> Psalm 8:2 NASB

child

Are you, or do you know, a parent who is teaching a child to pray? Listen to the child express thoughts in prayer. Little voices pray expecting God to hear their hearts and meet their needs. Listen and learn what a child can teach you.

Thank you, God, for my doll. God provides. Be grateful. *I have a boo-boo. Make it better.* Trust God. *Help me be nicer to my brother.* Believe that God can make a difference. *Thanks for listening, God. I'm better now.* Go to God when you need comfort. Pray from your heart. Be confident that God is listening.

≫ Buy a book of children's prayers. Think about the simplicity of childlike prayer, and express your thoughts and concerns to God in a similar simple manner.

#51

Catch a Glimpse of God

Rainbows in the clouds give a brief and otherwise invisible glimpse of colorful light in the sky. In the Bible, a rainbow is a promise from God made to Noah. A rainbow symbolizes God's promise made visible. To pray is to expect to see a rainbow—a brief glimpse of God's love shining through the clouds of circumstances in your life.

Whether you are weathering a storm or standing in a shower of blessings, God wants to reveal his love and promises for you. Make every prayer a request to catch a glimpse of God at work in you. Ask God to show you a rainbow.

catch

Bless me, O my Father, bless me, all my inner life renew. Now look down in love upon me. Let me catch a glimpse of you.

Author Unknown

≫ Hang a picture of a rainbow where you can see it every day. Thank God for every little glimpse of him in your life.

#52
Pray a Psalm

> *I will thank you,*
> *LORD, with all my*
> *heart; I will tell of*
> *all the marvelous*
> *things you have done.*
> *I will be filled with*
> *joy because of you.*
> *I will sing praises*
> *to your name,*
> *O Most High.*
>
> Psalm 9:1–2 NLT

psalm

Parallelism is a Hebraic poetic device found in many psalms. Sharing thoughts about his heart for worship, the psalmist wrote: "I will thank you, LORD, with all my heart" (Psalm 9:1 NLT), and then touched on the same thought again in the next verse, "I will be filled with joy because of you." Declare your own heart for worship by praying psalms.

As you pray psalms, pretend you are riding a carousel of praise, and travel around one thought to another. Let the words touch you with each pass. Like the music of a carousel, ask that each prayer of praise be a song of joyful music to God's ears.

≫ Be a psalmist. Write down your thoughts about God. Say them in more than one way. Pray your own psalm to God.

#53

Be Grateful for Grace

A supervisor explained to an employee their company's downsizing plan and said that they both should look for new jobs. The employee's response surprised the supervisor. She said, "I've reached the point in my life where I no longer say, 'Now what?' I am so sure of God's grace I just say, 'So what.' "

Know God is in control. Think about ways he works in your life for your good. Trust that he is moving now in ways you cannot see. Thank him that you can say "so what" in your circumstances. Express trust in him who knows what the future holds for you.

grace

The grace of God is sufficient for all our needs, for every problem, and for every difficulty, for every broken heart and for every human sorrow.

Peter Marshall

≫ Read Romans 8:28. Make it your personal prayer: "[I] know that all things work together for good to [me because I] love God" (NKJV).

#54

Reach Across Time

> There is...a time
> for every purpose
> under heaven
>
> Ecclesiastes 3:1 NKJV

time

There are stories of people waking up in the night to pray for missionaries or people who live far away, only to discover later that the person for whom they were praying really needed their prayers. Tomorrow in one time zone is still yesterday in another. Prayer reaches across time and space. Believe that God can use your prayer of now for yesterday or tomorrow.

The next time you wake up unexpectedly in the night, say a prayer. Pray for a struggling farmer in Kenya or a hungry child in Afghanistan. Pray as God leads. Then rest again in the knowledge that God heard your prayers.

≫ Whenever you wake in the night, pray especially for those who are serving your country.

#55

Get Your Exercise

Just as climbing stairs is good physical exercise for the heart, so also is taking a step toward God through prayer because it brings a greater spiritual well-being to your life. Each prayer is an exercise of faith. Faith grows stronger through prayer. Begin today to improve your spiritual life.

Get started by making daily prayer part of your routine. To climb stairs, you put one foot in front of the other. In prayer, you speak with God one prayer at a time. As a stair lifts you up one step to the next, ask God to help you envision each prayer lifting your heart a little closer to him.

exercise

> *Take the first step in faith. You don't have to see the whole staircase — just take the first step of faith.*
>
> Martin Luther King Jr.

≫ Do a good thing for your body. Take the stairs instead of the elevator. Pray as you climb the stairs. It will be good for your spirit.

#56

Believe in a Coming Spring

> *Whatever things you ask when you pray, believe that you receive them, and you will have them.*
>
> Mark 11:24 NKJV

spring

In autumn, plant a flowering bulb you'd enjoy seeing come to life the next spring: daffodils, tulips, or something else that grows well in your area. While you plant, talk to God about a request for your life that needs both time and prayer. Wait for springtime for your plant. Believe there will also be a spring for your prayer.

Know that when the time and conditions are right, the bulb will begin to grow and make its way to a new life aboveground. Think about the answer to your prayer in the same way. Tell God that you believe he will answer your prayer in his perfect time.

≫ Give a friend a flowering bulb like the one you planted. Ask the friend to pray with you and share the joy of spring together.

#57

Ask a Silly Question

Why do you think that God made giraffes? Funny faces, blotchy fur, and stiltlike legs give them an almost comical appearance. Just to see one makes people smile. Is it silly to wonder just why God chose to make this strange animal? Never be afraid to ask God anything, even what you might think is a "silly" question.

Go ahead and ask why God made giraffes or moose or porcupines, or ask him any other question you have. Any question that leads you to talk to him is a wise question. Find joy in any question that comes from a desire to know God.

ask

> *Find joy in everything that leads to God.*
>
> Saint Theresa of Avila

≫ Make a list of questions you want to ask God. See what God teaches you through your silly questions.

#58

Pray Anytime and Anywhere

Pray all the time.

1 Thessalonians 5:17
MSG

anytime

When you talk to God, do you feel you must empty your mind of distractions and go to a quiet place? A time of quiet is good and can be refreshing, but it is not the only time to pray. Prayer can happen anytime and anywhere. Begin and end your day today with prayer. Make today one long conversation with God.

Begin with "Dear God." Tell him why he is dear. Let the conversation flow freely. Thank him when you are thankful. Ask him for guidance. Tell him how you feel. Be sensitive to what he might want to teach you through the day. End today with "Amen."

>> Tomorrow write about your experience with praying anytime and anywhere. Ask God to help you make every day an anytime, anywhere day of prayer.

#59

Impact Others While You Are Here

An epitaph is a sentence summing up a person's life. It is a testament to who the person was and how he or she lived. While it may be possible to summarize the essence of your life in a few words, the impact of your life on those around you is not so easily measured.

Write a sentence today that sums up who you are and how you want to be remembered. Believe that your life is accomplishing more than just these few words. Thank God for your life. Ask him how you can make the most impact on other people while you are here.

impact

No one can sum up what God is able to accomplish through one solitary life, wholly yielded, adjusted, and obedient to him.

D. L. Moody

≫ Visit a cemetery and honor the life and memory of someone you love. Thank God for the way the person's life affected you.

#60
Make a Difference Today

> *Let's see how inventive we can be in encouraging love and helping out.*
>
> Hebrews 10:24 MSG

difference

A prayerful volunteer delivered meals to the elderly and took a few extra minutes at each home just to chat. The woman knew that many recipients would not have anyone else to talk to that day. She prayed that her few extra minutes of conversation would make a difference in a lonely person's day.

Make a difference in someone's life today. Ask God to place a lonely person in your path. Take a few minutes to chat to a store clerk, your hairdresser, or the postal delivery person. Be sensitive to the way people feel. Offer encouraging words. Ask God to help you make a difference in someone's day.

≫ Visit a nursing home. Ask who might not receive visitors. Ask God to show you something kind you can do for this person.

#61

Ask for a Greater Measure

A little boy said to his mother, "God is 5' 9" tall." Curious to understand his thinking, his mother asked how he knew. He answered, "Because that's how big my daddy is." Like that child, it's natural to measure God's greatness in terms you understand. Think about God today with a different kind of measure—the measure of your own heart.

God is as large to you as your own understanding. Be challenged by the greatness of God. Ask him to expand your understanding. Desire to accommodate more of who he is and who he can be through you. Ask God to increase the measure of your heart.

ask

> *Prayer enlarges the heart until it is capable of containing God's gift of himself.*
>
> Mother Teresa

>> Accept a new challenge to serve God in a way you haven't before. Enlarge your understanding of God's love at work through you.

#62

Carry Someone's Burden

> *Help carry one another's burdens, and in this way you will obey the law of Christ.*
>
> Galatians 6:2 GNT

carry

Do you have a friend who is facing a difficulty? Call your friend and say that you are going to carry the burden today in prayer. Ask your friend for a specific prayer you can pray. Invite the friend to picture giving the burden to you to carry. Then encourage the person to just leave the difficulty with God today as you pray.

Bear your friend's burden in prayer. Bring your petitions to God throughout the day. As you do, ask God to make your friend feel that the load is lighter because someone loves and cares enough to help carry it.

>> Ask God to show you how to lighten the load through something you can do in addition to prayer. Put your prayer into action.

#63

Be Short and Sweet

What do you or the person you are praying for really need most today? Try praying one-word prayers for yourself and others. Humbly tell God in one word what is on your heart. Let the word speak what you most need God's help with—perhaps *health, time,* or *compassion.* Or let the word speak someone's name. Do you need wisdom? Then say, "Wisdom."

The best communication is sometimes only a few words. Speak to the core of the matter. Even in prayer, one word can best express your need before God. When the need fits, be short and sweet in prayer.

short

> *Prayer should be short, without giving God Almighty reasons why he should grant this or that; he knows best what is good for us.*
>
> John Selden

>> Pray one-word prayers with your friends or family. Let each person contribute a one-word request for someone's need.

create

101 ways to

listen

trust

pretend

reach

talk to God

begin

plant

wait

#64

Develop a Heart Habit

> *We first make our habits, then our habits make us.*
>
> John Dryden

habit

A little girl often slept with her grandmother, even after the grandmother developed Alzheimer's disease. The two would lie in bed and talk until Grandma said, "It's time to pray." One night Grandma forgot they had already prayed and said again, "It's time to pray." They prayed many times before falling asleep.

For this grandmother, prayer was a habit. Even a disease could not stop her from a lifelong practice. Let prayer become a lifelong habit for you. Ask God for a prayer habit so well ingrained that even if your mind no longer functions well, you'll pray because your heart tells you to.

>> A habit is something you do with such regularity that it becomes almost instinctual. Decide what prayer habit you want to form, set the time and place, and begin.

#65
Make Delightful Lists

From top-ten lists to to-do lists, people seem to enjoy making lists. Checking off activities and events as they happen is satisfying. Make two lists today. Make a list of ways you can delight yourself in God, and then make another list of requests you'd take great delight in God's answering.

To delight in God means to understand and take joy in the things that matter to him. When making requests to God, ask him to help you pray for things that please him. Check off your request list as you receive answers to your prayers. Thank God as he gives you the desires of your heart.

lists

> *Do what the LORD wants, and he will give you your heart's desire.*
>
> Psalm 37:4 CEV

>> Read God's top ten rules for living from Exodus 20:7–17.
Ask God if you are following his list for living a life that pleases him.

#66

Have a Split Conversation

Prayer is not monologue, but dialogue; God's voice is the essential part. Listening to God's voice is the secret of the assurance that he will listen to mine.

Andrew Murray

split

Do you have a difficult person to face? Pray before you face him or her. Go with confidence that God goes with you. Make the conversation a three-way dialogue. As you speak to the person with your mouth, talk to God from your heart.

Ask God for wisdom as you speak. Request that he help the other person to be receptive. Listen for God's guidance before you speak. Ask God to show you how the conversation can be the catalyst for his will to be done in both you and the other person. As you hear with your ears, listen also with your heart.

≫ Make a list of difficult people you deal with in life. Pray good things for them. Pray that God will help resolve whatever may be troubling them.

#67

Give God Your Life Goals

Life is short. Consider the things you want to do in life. Include everything from having a family to taking a vacation in Bermuda to climbing Mount Everest. Write out your goals. Make them as detailed as you understand them today. Open your mind to every possibility, and then give God your goals.

Make pleasing God your number one goal. Look at the goals that are priorities to you. Separate the important to-do's from the would-like to-do's. Formulate your plans, but be willing to change a goal as God leads you. Ask God to lead you as you live his priorities.

goals

Always let him lead you, and he will clear the road for you to follow.

Proverbs 3:6 CEV

≫ As you complete God's priorities for you, check off your list. When you accomplish them all, ask for a new list.

#68
Take a Cleansing Bath

> *Wash your face every morning in a bath of praise.*
>
> Charles Spurgeon

bath

Do you shower or bathe in the morning? Let your shower or bath become a time to offer God prayers of cleansing and praise. Cleansing prayer allows you to ask God's forgiveness for something you've done or his help in forgiving someone who's wronged you. A prayer of cleansing often leads to a prayer of praise.

If you feel bad about something you said, know that God cleans up dirt and messes better than anyone. If someone hurt you, let your prayer rinse the hurt away. Pray to wash painful residue from your spirit. Praise God for his mercies that are new every morning.

≫ Sing a song of praise as you shower or bathe.

#69

Release Your Worries

Are you worried about an issue in life? Do you sometimes allow worry to choke your ability to enjoy life at all? Think of prayer as a way to release your anxieties to God one worry at a time. Like a balloon rising in the clouds, envision each anxious thought drifting toward heaven as you pray.

Is there really something you can do? If so, ask God to help you do it. If not, pretend to stand in a field of flowers and release your balloons to God. Ask him to help you be like a flower in the field with no worries today.

release

Which of you by worrying can add a single hour to his life's span? If then you cannot do even a very little thing, why do you worry about other matters? Consider the lilies, how they grow: they neither toil nor spin.

Luke 12:25–27 NASB

≫ Do something today that you love to do. Exchange worry for a day of joy.

#70

Find a New Way

> Let this be
> your chief object
> in prayer,
> to realize the
> presence of your
> Heavenly Father.
>
> Andrew Murray

way

Do you go to a traditional church? A contemporary church? A liturgical church? A temple? Plan this week to experience something different. Attend a different house of worship than you usually do. Be open to how others approach God in prayer. Look for new ways to get to know God.

Intimate time with God is not about the music, preaching, liturgy, or anything else. Each worship element is designed to draw your heart and mind into a time of focus on God. Allow new experiences to make a difference in your focus. Ask God for a new way to get to know him.

≫ Discuss the differences in worship with people who worship in a different way. Encourage people to share why they choose to worship as they do.

#71

Share a Gift of Grace

During the flurry of holiday preparations, take time to prepare a special gift for yourself and others at Christmas. Fill a box with Bible verses about God's grace, spending time to carefully and lovingly select the verses. Wrap the box as a special gift, and place it under the tree.

On Christmas morning, explain that you are unwrapping a gift that cannot be seen, but one that you've experienced. The gift is God's grace. Explain how God's grace has made a difference in your life. Pass the box around. Encourage everyone to take a Scripture. Offer a prayer of thanks for God's gift of grace.

grace

Thanks be to God for His indescribable gift!

2 Corinthians 9:15
NASB

≫ Look up the word *grace* in a Bible concordance to locate the verses about grace.

#72

Learn from Your Experience

Prayer is a climbing up of the heart into God. None can believe how powerful prayer is, and what it is able to effect, but those who learned it by experience.

Martin Luther

learn

A prayer journal is a tool many people use in learning to pray. Taking a few minutes each day—or even each week—to write down insights gained can be encouraging and inspiring. A prayer journal does not have to be fancy. A spiral notebook will do. Journaling teaches you about prayer through your own experience.

One of the joys of a prayer journal is to look back on the past and see the many ways God answers prayer. Ask God to help you learn through your journal. Be faithful in your prayers. Be faithful in your journaling. See what you can learn from your own experience.

≫ Keep a journal for a month, and then look back over the pages. See what God can teach you through journaling.

#73
Imagine Heaven

Heaven is one of God's gifts. Consider all that you know about heaven. Read about heaven's description in the Bible: Heaven is real. It is forever. There will be no more sorrow. You will see God. Picture yourself in heaven. Think about what is known.

Then, imagine what you don't know. Will you fly around? Will you know people who have arrived ahead of you? Can you do things there you always wished you could do here? Go ahead—imagine. Enjoy the mystery. Thank God for what you know about heaven and for the surprises that he will reveal to you when you experience it for yourself.

imagine

Beloved, now we are children of God, and it has not appeared as yet what we will be. We know that when He appears, we will be like Him, because we will see Him just as He is.

1 John 3:2 NASB

≫ Listen to the song "I Can Only Imagine" by Mercy Me. Imagine your own response to seeing God.

#74

Pray Like Hannah

When there is a matter that requires definite prayer, pray until you believe God and until you can thank him for his answer.

Hannah Whitall Smith

hannah

Do you have a desire you pray for? The Bible tells the story of Hannah, a young woman who had one desire—to have a child. She prayed passionately and willingly offered to dedicate the child to God if he granted her prayer. God gave her a son. When the child was old enough, her desire became to take her son to the temple to serve.

Pray like Hannah when you talk to God about a desire of your heart. Speak your deepest longing. Be willing to dedicate the result to him. Tell God you desire the outcome of your prayer to best serve his purposes for you.

≫ Think of a prayer God has answered. How did his answer change your life? How did it change the lives of other people? Consider how his answer helped serve his purpose for you.

#75

Get a Whiff and Pray

The aroma of coffee brewing in the morning is a wake-up call and an enticement to start the day for many people. During the day, a cup of coffee is an invitation to take a break, have a conversation, or sit down and discuss business. Let the aroma of coffee also remind you to talk to God.

Breathe in God's presence, and relax when you smell coffee. Enjoy a quick or an intimate conversation with him. Take care of important personal prayer business. Wake up to a cup and a prayer. Pray whenever you get a whiff of coffee during the day.

aroma

Continue praying, keeping alert, and always thanking God.

Colossians 4:2 NCV

≫ Try a new flavor of coffee. Thank God for the variety of good things he has given you to enjoy.

#76

Stand Together

> *It brings comfort to have companions in whatever happens.*
>
> Saint John Chrysostom

stand

A family lost their beloved mother. Though they had never prayed together before, one family member said, "I think we should pray." Hesitantly, they gathered in a circle and held hands. One by one, each prayed from the heart. Then something happened. A peace soon enveloped the room. Tears of grief became tears of love and encouragement for one another. They stood together, they prayed together, and God supported them.

Take the hands of those you love. Pray together about things concerning you. Let the strength of God sustain you. Pray together to stand strong in unity through whatever you face. Stand together in prayer.

≫ Gather loved ones for a meal or a family game of sports. Ask everyone to make a circle of prayer, and thank God for the gift of family.

#77

Do Your Work for God

On Monday, are you already looking forward to the weekend? If you discover that's the way you feel more often than not, stop and ask God to change the way you respond to the workplace. Rekindle your enthusiastic spirit by focusing on whom you really serve. Do your job as if you are working for God.

Ask how God sees you at work. Are you doing the best you can? Is it possible to see the greater good your job does? Talk to God and ask him to help you see the importance of your work. Serve him through your job. Be God's excellent employee. Be positive at work.

> work

> *Do your work with enthusiasm. Work as if you were serving the Lord, not as if you were serving only men and women.*
>
> Ephesians 6:7 NCV

≫ You influence not only your own attitude but the attitudes of your coworkers as well. Think of at least one positive way you can demonstrate a good attitude at work.

#78

Get in Rhythm

> *The soul is brought by love to delight in meditation alone.*
>
> Marguerite Porete

rhythm

One can describe intimacy as two people sharing one heartbeat. In the world of medicine, surgeons describe what happens when two hearts laid side by side on a table touch each other. After a minute or two they will begin to beat in unison. Sharing God's heartbeat is possible. Discover how to be intimate with him through prayer.

Discovering God's rhythm happens when you desire a close relationship with him. Lay your heart on the table. Let the heart of God touch yours. Pray for intimacy with God. Ask him to bring your heart and life in rhythm with his heartbeat.

≫ Pack a brown-bag picnic lunch, head for a nearby park or natural area, and give yourself an impromptu personal retreat to get yourself in sync with God's rhythm.

#79

Inspire an Everyday Hero

Everyday heroes are people who demonstrate extraordinary courage in difficult situations. Merriam-Webster defines *courage* as "mental or moral strength to venture, persevere, and withstand danger, fear, or difficulty." *Courage* is part of the word *encourage*. To encourage is to inspire with courage and hope.

Do you know people who are facing difficulties today? How are they doing? Do you admire how they are handling the situation they face? Are they fighting bravely, responding with humor, or just quietly accepting their situation? Inspire someone with hope. Encourage others with love. Make each situation a matter for your prayers every day.

inspire

Is anything too hard for the LORD? No!

Genesis 18:14 NCV

≫ Ask for God's wisdom and strength for illness, loss, or whatever your everyday hero may face. Look for a Bible verse to pray, too.

delight

101 ways to

do

look

formulate

cleanse

talk to God

release

exchange

allow

#80

Stand Up for Justice

> *The pearl of justice is found in the heart of mercy.*
>
> Saint Catherine of Siena

stand

Jackie Robinson, a ballplayer who helped break down the barrier of racism in baseball, dropped the ball once on his home field. The crowd hissed and screamed at him. One of his white teammates walked over to stand beside Robinson. Together they stood and faced the crowd. The stands became quiet.

In the game of life, be a person who stands with others to face adversity. Have a heart to see when another person suffers injustice. Pray for guidance in knowing how to help. Ask God to help you know when to stand up for a person in need and to face the crowd.

>> Watch a television program about courtroom justice. Pray that justice will be served and all participants find peace in the process.

#81

Give Legs to God's Love

A sad old man sat alone eating a Thanksgiving dinner provided by a local charity. One perceptive volunteer talked with him. After chatting awhile, he rewarded her with a smile and a hug. "Why do you do this?" the man asked. She answered, "Because God wants me to show his love by helping others." The man looked at her gratefully and said, "Thank you for being God's legs."

Pray to discover a new way to be charitable, to act as God's legs. Investigate a need and a charity that meets that need. Be open to ways to share God's love and be his legs.

legs

> *Now abide faith, hope, love, these three; but the greatest of these is love.*
>
> 1 Corinthians 13:13
> NKJV

≫ Commit to a short-term volunteer job you've never done before at a church or a charity.

#82

Listen for the Right Time

> Speak, Lord, for
> Thy Servant
> heareth. Grant
> us ears to hear,
> eyes to see, wills
> to obey, hearts
> to love.
>
> Christina Rossetti

listen

Kairos is a Greek word that translates as "right time." The urge to pray may come when God instructs you that your prayer can make a difference. Prayer like this is not something you will experience every day. Join others who respond to inner prompting and who, when they pray, discover the urge was given for a reason.

Be sensitive to times when you feel the urge to pray. Pray for the person who comes to your mind. Pray a specific request if you feel compelled to do so. Ask God to help you to listen for the right time and to pray for the right reason.

≫ Focus in prayer on a friend's or loved one's need today instead of on your own need.

#83

Be Willing to Give

Everyone hopes to live a long, healthy life. But tomorrow is never guaranteed. A decision today to be an organ donor could give someone you don't know many more tomorrows. Ask God if he wants you to be willing to give a gift of life to someone else, even if you never become a donor.

Envision a son or a daughter receiving your kidney. Consider a husband who will die without a new heart. Imagine a mother who needs a liver. The promise of eternity is a gift from God for your life. Pray about giving the gift from your body that could give someone life.

give

You formed my inward parts; You wove me in my mother's womb. I will give thanks to You, for I am fearfully and wonderfully made.

Psalm 139:13–14
NASB

≫ Picture in your mind a major organ as it functions in your body. Thank God for your body and the health you have today.

#84

Fill Someone's Shoes

> *True love does not come from what we receive but from what we give.*
>
> Saint John Chrysostomos

fill

A woman cherished the thoughtful cards her mother-in-law sent for birthdays and other family occasions, always with a personal note. Sadly, her mother-in-law died. But when the grieving woman went to the mailbox on her birthday, she discovered a card—sent by her father-in-law. Touched deeply by the gesture, she tearfully thanked him for filling his wife's shoes.

Do you know someone who has lost a family member? Offer the family the gift of doing something the loved one would have done if he or she were still here. Ask God to show you an opportunity or gesture to comfort someone who has suffered a loss. Fill someone's shoes.

>> Volunteer at a hospice center. Look for ways to minister to people who are in distress for their ill loved ones.

#85

Host a "Care Aware" Party

Give your next party a different kind of theme. Think about a need that you could meet in your community. Consider what party guests could do to care for others, or what they could bring for the benefit of others. Design a party to encourage others to give time or money. Offer your party to God as a gift.

Make the party fun. Design invitations to reflect the theme. Suggest items to give for an agency or an activity to do for a cause. Consider contests or games to encourage giving or doing. Thank God for a creative opportunity to show love to others because he loves you.

host

We love because God first loved us.

1 John 4:19 NCV

>> Before you do anything, pray first that your efforts will be God-honoring, then direct your energy where it is most needed.

#86

Try a Sticky-Note Method

Any method, absolutely any method, is your method if you find it opens the door toward heaven and helps you make contact with God.

Frank Laubach

sticky-note

A television commercial for a brand of sticky-notes shows a squirrel taking the notes off an office desk. Inside a tree, the camera shows rows of sticky-notes, supposedly written to remind the squirrel where to find his treasures. Take a good idea from this ad. Buy some sticky-notes and use them to remember to pray.

Write things or people's names to pray for on them. Post them in conspicuous places. A squirrel may not really need a note to remember where his treasures are. But a sticky-note may serve to remind you what a treasure you have in prayer. See a note. Say a prayer.

≫ Do you have a prayer request you want to share with someone else? Give a sticky-note with your request written on it to help him or her remember to pray for your need.

#87

Be Inspired by Faith Heroes

Amy Carmichael rescued children destined to be temple prostitutes in India. Gladys Alward faced angry prisoners in China. Dwight Moody helped raise Chicago from both physical and spiritual ashes. All were people who prayed for God's provision to meet their needs. See what a hero of faith can teach you. Discover how people of the past talked to God. Learn how prayer made all the difference.

Amy Carmichael demonstrated compassion. Pray for compassion. Gladys Alward found courage in prayer. Pray for courage. Dwight Moody trusted God to provide direction for his life. Pray that you, too, can trust God.

heroes

Consider what I say, for the Lord will give you understanding in everything.

2 Timothy 2:7 NASB

≫ Find and read a book about a hero of faith. There are many, but here are a few to consider: Jim Elliot, Mary Slessor, Billy Graham, Corrie ten Boom, Frederick Douglass.

#88

Take a Prayer Walk

He walks with me, and he talks with me, and he tells me I am his own, and the joy we share as we tarry there, none other has ever known.

C. Austin Miles

w a l k

Go on a walk with a larger purpose in mind than just getting some physical exercise. Walk through a neighborhood or a park and pray as you go. With every step, look for things to pray for and to pray about. Do you see people? Pray that God would become as real to them as he is to you. Is the sun shining? Thank God for a beautiful day.

Now imagine that God is walking with you. (He is.) Go back the same way you came. Ask him to show you things you missed along the way. Tell God how much you enjoy walking and talking together.

>> Sit in the grass. Notice the usually unseen life—crawling insects in the grass. Ask God for eyes to trust his unseen movements through your prayers.

#89

Hold Someone's Hand

Ecclesiastes 4:9, 12 reads, "You are better off to have a friend than to be all alone. . . . 'A rope made from three strands of cord is hard to break'" (CEV). In prayer, there are times when two are better than one. Hold someone's hand in prayer. Know God's presence in a prayer relationship between two people is the third strand.

Reach for the hand of your spouse. Discover new intimacy through prayer. Reach for the hand of a friend. Strengthen your relationship through prayer. Feel the difference that holding the hand of someone you love makes. Experience the strength of three strands in prayer together.

hold

Whenever two or three of you come together in my name, I am there with you.

Matthew 18:20 CEV

≫ Make a three-strand prayer cord that you can give as a gift to your prayer partner. Tell him or her what the strands represent to you.

#90

Take on a Tough Issue

> *God, give us grace to accept with serenity the things that cannot be changed, courage to change the things which should be changed, and the wisdom to distinguish the one from the other.*
>
> Reinhold Niebuhr

issue

Is there an injustice that disturbs you? Are you sad because of a situation that should be changed? What issue or cause ignites passion in you? Take on the tough issues in prayer. Ask for divine guidance in tackling a problem. Fight injustice in the world. Make a difference through prayer.

Begin by asking God how to pray. Seek to understand the issue as best you can. Educate yourself about what others are doing to resolve the problem. Based on what you learn, make your prayers specific. Ask God to show you the best way to take on a tough issue. Be passionate in your prayers.

≫ Do you hate child abuse? Become a Court Appointed Special Advocate (CASA) volunteer. Help to tackle this or other issues important to you.

#91

Pray As You Pay

Everything you have belongs to God. He wants you to trust him with your finances. He knows what your needs are. Before you calculate your budget, first set aside what you are going to give God. Be faithful to give something for God's work in the world.

Are there sometimes more bills than money? Pray before you sit down with your checkbook. Look at your bills. Ask if you are spending God's money wisely. Evaluate the difference between a want and a need. Give to God first. Pay what is due. And then trust God for your needs. Pray as you pay.

More than anything else, put God's work first and do what he wants. Then the other things will be yours as well.

Matthew 6:33 CEV

≫ Take a class on managing or investing your money. Ask God to help you understand how to plan financial matters wisely.

#92
Ask for a Life Verse

He spoke a Book and lives in His spoken words, constantly speaking His words and causing the power of them to persist across the years.

A. W. Tozer

verse

The Bible speaks God's wisdom for living. A life verse is a Bible verse that speaks to an individual so strongly that it becomes a guiding daily influence. The verse may speak to an issue the individual faces or summarize the person's desire to trust in God's providence. Read the Bible to discover a verse that speaks so clearly that you know it is meant for you.

The Bible has been read by countless and continuing generations. It is a gift to everyone who seeks to understand God. Pray that he will show you your life verse. Let God speak his wisdom for your life through the Bible.

≫ Ask friends if they have a favorite or life verse. Ask them why the verse is important to them.

# #

Pray Your A

A is for altruism. *B* is for belief. *C* is for character. Pray for an altruistic spirit. Do something good for someone today and expect nothing in return. Belief is conviction that something is true. Pray today that you would live your convictions in all you do. Pray today that your good character would point someone to God.

Altruism, belief, character. Learning these ABC's is more than just acquiring knowledge about what they are. Living these ABC's takes daily lessons from God through prayer and daily application of the principles. Ask God to teach you as you learn and live your ABC's.

a b c

> *These are the qualities you need, and if you have them in abundance, they will make you active and effective in your knowledge of our Lord Jesus Christ.*
>
> 2 Peter 1:8 GNT

≫ Make up an acrostic for the word *belief*, an acrostic that describes what you believe to be true about God. Here's an example:
B-eautiful E-ternal L-oving I-ncredible E-verlasting F-riend—BELIEF.

#94

Ask for a Miracle

> *No one is ever surprised over what God does when he has faith in him.*
>
> Oswald Chambers

miracle

A writer once submitted a true story of faith to her publisher. The publisher sent it back with the comment that it was too unbelievable to be true. Do you have the joy of faith? A story that's too good to be true? From small miracles to large ones, God moves through prayers of faith in miraculous ways.

The miracle begins when you accept the reality of God. The God of all creation loves you. To communicate with him through prayer is a miracle. Ask God for your own story of faith. Ask God to begin a miraculous work in you.

>> Does your own faith story have a beginning? If not, begin one today. If you know when your story began, share your story with someone today.

#95

Pray Without Pretense

Discover the difference that complete honesty in prayer makes. The psalms express honest emotions in prayer—joy, sadness, despair, anger, and fear, to name a few. When the apostle Peter was drowning, Jesus responded to his short emotional prayer, "Lord, save me!" From the well of your emotions, when you strip all pretenses away, real prayer flows.

Are you as happy as one human being can be? Tell God. Are you unbelievably angry? Tell God. Did you just experience the deepest disappointment of your life? Tell God. In prayer, a genuine cry like "Lord, save me!" is a prayer God responds to.

pretense

I call out at the top of my lungs, "GOD! Answer! I'll do whatever you say."

Psalm 119:145 MSG

>> Read Psalm 100. Note such words as *joy* and *gladness* that express emotion. Ask yourself what deep-felt emotions you share with God.

stand

101 ways to

be

commit

join

donate

talk to God

picture

offer

design

#96
Count the Ways

How do I love thee? Let me count the ways.

Elizabeth Barrett Browning

count

How many ways are there to talk to God? The list is as varied as the people who live in the world. Each personality expresses his or her heart before God in many ways throughout the course of a lifetime. There are themes common to all. A conversation with God demonstrates your love for God.

How do you talk to God? Make your own list. Make it through experience. Do prayer. Say prayer. Sing prayer. Write prayer. Be prayer. Care through prayer. Ask God to help you discover all the ways you can demonstrate your love for him. Live a life of prayer.

≫ Focus on a different way you can talk to God each day. Ask him to teach you to live a life of prayer.

#97

Applaud God

If God is important in your life, your response to him in life will be his applause. Do you respond to him with enthusiasm or just a polite nod once in a while? Applaud God with more than a casual response. Live your life as resounding applause that honors him.

Give God the standing ovation he deserves in everything you do. Be genuinely enthusiastic about who he is. Say bravo to him for his power and for all he's given you. Adore him because you are his biggest fan. Share your excitement with others. Pray to live as God's applause.

applaud

Bravo, GOD, bravo! Gods and all angels shout, "Encore!" In awe before the glory, in awe before God's visible power. Stand at attention!

Psalm 29:1–2 MSG

≫ Pretend you are the president of God's fan club. Write him a fan letter. Tell him how glad you are that he is God and how happy you are to be his.

#98

Ask If Now Is the Time

If we are going to be or do anything for our Lord, now is the time.

Vance Havner

now

The biblical account of Esther tells the story of a queen who was in a position to save her people. Because to enter the king's court uninvited could have been a death sentence, she was reluctant to approach him. Her uncle's query—"Who knows if you were born for such a time as this?"—changed her mind. Esther's willingness to go saved her people.

Is there a situation you know that you are uniquely qualified to handle? Are you alone in a position to make a difference? Ask God if there is a task he has for you because you were made "for such a time as this."

>> Think about and pray for people in your life you influence because of who you are or what you do.

#99

Be Enriched Through Fasting

Remember people around the world in prayer who face hunger today. Rice is a staple food in many countries. Fast for a week by serving rice alone at one meal each day. Invite your family or a friend to do the same. Donate money you save by not buying food or eating out to a charity.

After the week is over, ask God to help you be sensitive to hungry people in your area. Volunteer to help in a soup kitchen. Gather food for a food pantry. Honor God through your actions. Ask God for a generous spirit to share your blessings and bounty with others.

A generous person will be enriched.

Proverbs 11:25
NRSV

>> Investigate an organization and pray about sponsoring children or families in another country. Pray about making a monthly commitment to help someone in need.

#100

State Your Family's Purpose

Do all the good you can, by all the means you can, in all the ways you can, in all the places you can, at all the times you can, to all the people you can, as long as ever you can.

John Wesley

purpose

A mission statement declares a purpose and ways to accomplish the stated purpose. Do you have a family mission statement? Do you know what you hope your family will accomplish in life and how you as a family will do it? Would your family's mission statement reflect God's plan for you?

Ask God to help you evaluate your family life. Are you teaching your children to love God and help others? What are the most important things you do together? Ask God to help you discover his plan and purpose for your family. Write a purpose statement and three ways to accomplish your purpose.

≫ Challenge families you know to consider not only individual goals but also family goals. Discuss why families should have a mission statement.

#101

Look to the Morning Star

Ask God to be your light and hope. Like twinkling lights in the night sky, each time you talk to God your prayers shine a gleam of light on your path. The brightest star, called the morning star, is a symbol of hope because it appears in the darkest hour just before dawn. In the Bible, Jesus says he is the Morning Star, eternal hope.

Look to the Morning Star. God is the hope of eternity to those who believe. Do you have the light of eternal hope? Invite the light of his love to come be a part of you. Then thank him for being your hope and everlasting light.

star

The LORD will be your everlasting light, and your God will be your glory.

Isaiah 60:19 NIV

≫ Rejoice that the God of the universe hears and answers more prayers in your lifetime than there are stars in the sky.

*Let the Spirit of God lead us
into the intent of God's heart.*

Watchman Nee